UNDEFEATABLE SPIRIT

The story of 11 days, of Albert, and the lads from the yards.
The Norfolk Regiment. 1909-1919.

NIGEL CUSHION

Undefeatable Spirit. The story of 11 days, of Albert, and the lads from the yards. The Norfolk Regiment. 1909-1919.

Published by Nelsonspirit Publishing, a trading name of Nelsonspirit Limited. Designed, typeset and printed by Hollinger Print, Norwich, England. www.hollinger.co.uk. Another book published by Nelsonspirit Publishing by Nigel Cushion is: Action Stations. A field manual on stress for high performers and leaders. © Nigel Cushion 2019.

A CIP record for this book is available from the British Library.
978-1-9160039-1-0

Front cover: The survivors of the 350 yard dash, the dash in the desert. The Norfolk Battalion bayonet charge at Shaiba, Mesopotamia 1915. Picture taken south of Ctesiphon. Albert is second row, kneeling fifth from the left. © Neil Storey Archive.

DEDICATION

This book is for the grandchildren, of the grandchildren, of the boys from Kut.

It is dedicated to Albert and all the lads from the Norwich yards, and of the Norfolk Regiment ... all good soldiers and all good men, of undefeatable spirit.

2 NORFOLK on Parade in Norwich, on their return home, 1919.

"They welcomed us back to Norwich, the real promised land;
They marched us up to City Hall, flags waving in their hand.
They called us heroes, they said they'd done the sums;
They said of all the holy boys, we were the lucky ones."

PREFACE

This is a story of eleven days:

A story of Albert and lads from the yards, the slums of Norwich, who left home as boys with nothing.

A story of a forgotten battalion, in a forgotten theatre of the First World War, fighting against a ferocious enemy, in one of the most hostile and dangerous environments on earth.

A story of fun and comradeship, with boys who joined up together, full of excitement and hope for a great adventure.

A story of great leadership, achievement and victory, including one of the last battalion bayonet charges in history, into machine gun fire, led by an Officer carrying only a sword.

A story of discipline, professionalism and courage of the British and Indian troops, who in atrocious conditions, and against huge odds, captured more ground for least casualties, proving they were the right of the line, "the best of the best".

A story of the longest siege in British military history and the biggest British surrender since Yorktown.

A story of dysentery, cholera, plague, typhus, beriberi, sand-fly, malaria, heatstroke, scurvy, sniping, shooting, bombing, starvation, surrender, neglect, mistreatment, atrocities, and survival.

A story a of a thousand mile death march through the desert ending at a concentration camp.

A story where only one in ten men came home to live a good life.

A story that for a hundred years has not been told.

A story of Albert and lads from the yards, the slums of Norwich, who left home as boys with nothing, but who came home as men with "something" .... Undefeatable Spirit.

CONTENTS

TESTIMONIES

"Thank you so much for giving me a copy of your book about your grandfather's experiences in World War One. I have thoroughly enjoyed reading it. The concept of eleven days within that extraordinary ten years is brilliant. The pride for Norfolk shines through on every page. What a remarkable man - brilliantly portrayed".

General The Lord Dannatt GCB, CBE, MC, DL.
Former Chief of The General Staff (Head of The British Army).

"A highly readable account drawn from one of the lesser known campaigns of the Great War. Nigel Cushion brings this personal story of a Norfolk family to life, highlighting the lasting effects of military service on people's lives, many of which still apply today."

Maj. Gen (Ret'd) Greg Smith CB QVRM TD. Norfolkman.
Former Assistant Chief of the Defence Staff (Reserves & Cadets).

"A superb read that cleverly brings to life the lot of a Norfolk soldier in a part of the world that many of today's soldiers would recognise. Through this colourful story, you get a real sense of the relationships that sit at heart of a fighting force and which underpin the all-important esprit de corps. The voices of these soldiers come alive on the pages. A piece of military history forever captured in a great story by Nigel Cushion."

Brig. James Woodham CBE, MC. Norfolkman. Former Commanding Officer 1 R ANGLIAN 2008-2011, and Commander 7th Armoured Brigade 'The Desert Rats' 2013-2015.

"What a fascinating account. Well done Nigel Cushion for researching a forgotten part of our local history. Little did Albert and his comrades know, that nearly one hundred years later, in 2005, the young men of Norfolk would return to Shaiba for an operational deployment with 1st Battalion, Royal Anglian Regiment, in the aftermath of the Second Gulf War. While many things have changed, the demands of fighting in the desert, leadership and spirit remain timeless."
Lt Col. (Ret'd) Mark Nicholas MBE. Norfolkman. Chairman of the Royal Norfolk Regimental Association and County Colonel for Norfolk. Former A (Norfolk) Company, 1 R ANGLIAN, Iraq 2005.

"A great book, an epic story. This is the incredibly evocative tale of Norfolk boys on a remarkable endeavour, vividly envisioned by Norfolkman Nigel Cushion, the grandson of one of the lads."
Major Robert Smit. Norfolkman. Apache Pilot in the Army Air Corps. Former Platoon Commander and Company 2IC, A (Norfolk) Company, 1 R ANGLIAN, 2001-2007, including Iraq and Afghanistan.

"In 2008, whilst serving with the 2nd Battalion, The Royal Anglian Regiment, I had the honour of treading the same 'hot, flat and dirty' Shaiba ground that 2 NORFOLK did. Testament to Nigel's work, the sentiment and banter reflected throughout reminds me of my own similar thoughts – in the same places. After many amalgamations and reorganisation within the British Army, A (Norfolk) Coy, 1st Battalion, The Royal Anglian Regiment are essentially the modern-day representatives of The Royal Norfolk Regiment. We take our history seriously. Today, we still adorn the Britannia and call ourselves the 'Fighting Ninth'. The county link, pride and distinction we feel, contributes directly to the moral component of our fighting power. Our continuous endeavour to honour our glorious forebears is a great motivator and drives our esprit de corps; helping us to perform better on the modern battlefield."
Major Adam Mackness, Officer Commanding, A (Norfolk) Company, 1 R ANGLIAN, 2019.

"This book is great because it is written about the actual troops and what they had to endure at the front, not what the hierarchy supposed it to be like! Comparable with Bravo Two Zero, which was also written from the troops' perspective, and the 'c**k ups' of the intelligence services and management decisions. I thoroughly enjoyed it, and can't wait for the film. Unfortunately my former employers have advised that I should not advertise that I was anywhere, let alone the desert! I wish you all the success you deserve with this book."
Special Forces Operative in the Middle East 1973 - 1980.

"Reading histories, such as this, opens our minds to experiences of the past and allows us to relate them to the present and future. Personal histories, especially those written about the adversity and challenge of war allows us to create a personalised narrative that influences our very being."
Dan Browning, Head Teacher, BA (Hons), PGCE, NPQH, PCPS, FCMI.
Wymondham College, Norfolk.

"Thank you so much for sharing your Grandfather's story. The book was incredible and I thoroughly enjoyed it. Your story makes me proud to be from Norwich. I can't convey how grateful we are for the 2 NORFOLKs, who suffered greatly, but never lost their humour; servicemen like Albert Cushion, Bertie Cushion, RSM Charlie Aldridge, Mo and Smithy. The story is incredible. It made me laugh and cry the whole way through, but also feel proud of where I'm from."
Amy March, Student of History, Aged 18. Wymondham College, Norfolk.

INTRODUCTION

On the eleventh day of the eleventh month each year we are asked to remember "them". But how much do we really know about who "they" were? In 2018, on the one hundredth anniversary of the ending of The Great War, my brother and I became interested in finding out about our relatives who had fought in this war. Paul and I, as Cushion brothers living in Norwich today, were fascinated about what happened to the Cushion brothers two generations back, in 1914-18.

We knew that our grandad Albert Edward Cushion, had been in the war alongside his younger brother Bertie Cecil Cushion. The narrative passed down through the family was that "they went off to Gallipoli, Bertie Cecil got killed, Albert Edward (our grandad) came back, after spending two years a prisoner. They never talked about it". Like many families, that is all we knew.

After some initial research, we discovered that while Bertie Cecil did indeed serve and die in Gallipoli, Albert Edward his elder brother, was not in Gallipoli at all. We then became intrigued to piece together Albert's real story. It turned out that Albert did fight the Turks, but in Mesopotamia, modern day Iraq, in a forgotten part of the First World War. Albert had joined up as a professional soldier in 1909, when the employment prospects for the less well off in Norwich were limited. He had served in the 2nd Battalion of the Norfolk Regiment, part of the British Indian Army, and then in 1914 was sent to Mesopotamia. He saw significant and successful action in the desert, took part in one of the longest and worst sieges in British military history, resulting in the biggest surrender since Yorktown, was put on a thousand-mile death march, and ended up in a concentration camp in Turkey. We became fascinated about his journey from the perspective of a boy from Norwich, who was a private solder. How had he and his mates coped with all this, and what happened when they came home?

History is often told from the perspective of the rich and famous, about the generals and politicians. Albert was from the Norwich yards. The yards were where the poor of the city lived, although they would not have regarded themselves as coming from slums. They were the better off poor, the so called "working poor". How would this great adventure been experienced by a boy from the yards? The work of Danny Boyle inspired us to think about how the war might be viewed from the perspective of the common man. The images in 2018 of the portraits on the beaches being washed away by the tide, prompted us to see whether we could find any photographs of our grandad. Our interest was further stimulated when friends from Norfolk serving with the modern descendent military unit, 1 ROYAL ANGLIAN, came across a cemetery during the 2005 Iraq war. When these modern soldiers from 'A' (Norfolk) Company scraped the gravestones, they found the names of lads from the yards of Wymondham, Cromer, Yarmouth and Norwich, having died there in 1916. Recognising their family names they realised they had found their forebears – 2 NORFOLK, in this forgotten corner of a foreign field.

On the weekend of the hundredth anniversary of the end of the First World War, on 11th November 2018, my brother was outside Norwich City Hall, where the dead from Norwich were remembered by huge crowds. The civic hall contained boards of remembrance, naming those that had lost their lives fighting for King and Country, born in and around the Norwich area. After the playing of the Last Post, the civic hall began reading out the names of the Norwich boys that had fallen, this would take five hours to conclude. My brother stood with many others in silent reflection, as Bertie Cecil's name was read out. An event no doubt repeated in numerous cities and towns across the country that day.

Meanwhile my wife Nicki and I were visiting our son Jake at Durham University. That Sunday morning we found ourselves at the back of a packed cathedral, for the Remembrance Service. We had limited visibility, so my mind began to wander and I thought about Albert Edward and his mates in 2 NORFOLK. Again, we were asked "to remember them", but again, I had to admit that we did not really know "they" were.

I imagined what Albert Edward might say to Paul and I if he had been with us on that commemorative day, and I was moved to craft the poem "They", using Albert Edward's imagined voice. It is reproduced at the back of this book. On checking some of the historical details, we became further absorbed and fascinated to learn more. In 2019, we were able to talk to our Uncle Albert, now aged 91, to get first hand reflections on his father (Albert Edward), who we had never met. We wondered what a conversation might be like if we were to have a pint with our grandad now, and get him to talk to us about his adventures. As most bar conversations, this might well focus on him talking up his great adventures, and the laughs, into a few days of highlights. The idea of his imagined voice and fictionalised diary had been born, and reflecting on 11/11, the idea of telling his story through 11 days of his life.

So here it is. This diary is a fictionalised account, written in Albert's voice. I have done my best to get the historical facts, details, and the cultural norms of the time, right, but of course it remains fiction. The extraordinary events, outcomes and places are true. Much of the dialogue and "banter" is imagined, but it is based on records and research. Some of the characters mentioned are real, others are composites. I have toned down the language as it is likely that Albert would have used more Norfolk dialect and military slang than I have used, but a book of this nature would be unreadable to most. I have shown in brackets a translation where this is appropriate. I have also researched the literature, but very little of it exists, particularly after the Siege of Kut, which has made the research both challenging and fascinating. We will never know exactly what happened or how he and others really felt. You can only really know what it is like if you were there, but knowing Norfolk, my family, and the army, I have done my best to find a truth in a story that can stand up. While it remains a story, my acid test in writing, was whether I could look the ghosts of boys from Kut in the eye and they tell me that they recognise this story as theirs. Could I win their respect for what I have tried to do? Looking at the pictures of them - this would be a challenge indeed for me!

You will find that Chapter eight is blank. This is because due to the nature of it, there are no records, and I did not feel that I could ever imagine this chapter, and rather than writing something which is way off mark, out of respect for the boys, I have left this blank. This also acts as the "missing man" page.

We have found the story of Albert and the lads both interesting and inspirational. We hope you do too. One interesting finding was that the received wisdom, and we have been told this many times, that "they", the returning soldiers, "did not want to talk about it". We found this to be true, but we also found, uncomfortably, that those back home, the families, communities, businesses, politicians, government and the media, did not want to talk about it either. In my view those back home were not kind enough, nor did enough for the returning veterans. This made it unnecessarily hard for those coming back from the war, many of whom went straight into depression. This was the economic depression of the 1920s and 1930s, where many of the men who had fought in The Great War were starving on the street. It was also in some cases, mental health depression, where it was dealt with even less sympathetically than it is today.

We thought at a hundred years, it is about time that their inspirational story is told, of the forgotten theatre in Mesopotamia, of their adventures, of the fun they had, of the challenges they faced, and of the undefeatable spirit of the boys from the yards, who left as boys and came home as men. And if they are watching us a hundred years on, we say to them, they have been remembered. We salute their spirit, and they should know, it marches on.

Nigel Cushion

Grandson of Albert Edward Cushion
2019... a hundred years since the boys from the yards came home.

7983, Private Albert Edward Cushion.
The Norfolk Regiment. Joined up 1909, came home 1919.

1
THE YARDS TO THE BARRACKS

... the day I joined the right of the line.

My new pals. 1 NORFOLK in Barracks, Belfast 1909.
Albert is on the right of the line, second from right, standing.

"They said, you should join the army boy,
They said, the Norfolk's are for you;
Go you up to Britannia Barracks,
And your mates will be there too."

King Edward had just visited Norwich and there had been loads of soldiers on the streets. Me and my mates thought they looked great, and many had stories of their adventures in Africa and in far off places of empire. It captured my imagination. At nearly 18 years old, this seemed a world away from the dreary monotony of the boot factory at St Mary's or the Brewery which were my two options in life. I saw how hard my dad had worked, and how hard my grandad had worked, just to feed and clothe us. We did not think of ourselves as poor, but we did not have a lot. My grandad had spent his whole life as a basket weaver, and had just died having never left Norwich. My mother had also just passed away. My dad had taken a new wife, and we were about to have some step brothers and sisters, all living in a small house in Pyes Yard. His new wife was OK, but she was not our mum. I thought maybe this was the time I needed to leave the yards and go discover the world. My domestic and work prospects seemed unappealing, but the army seemed so exciting.

So, I joined up. I liked the army and the army seemed to like me. They looked after you, they clothed you, housed you, and gave you three meals a day. Where I came from this was heaven. And then you have loads of mates around you, many of whom I knew from the streets of Norwich. You had a bloody good laugh and ended most days at the bar having a few, well actually, lots of drinks. I loved the training, the discipline and the exercise and every time we marched about the battalion band was there playing - and they were bloody good. For a young man from my background, I had more than anyone I knew.

The day I remember was our first night in barracks, mainly for being introduced to two new things: one was the Officers, (called "The Toffs") and the other was called "Drinking Games". According to the Sergeants and the old sweats, the Officers usually fell into the following categories: the Twits, the Twats, and the Tidys. The Twits were upper class idiots, who basically ignored us. They were harmless and hopeless but generally OK, if you kept out of their way. The Twats were upper class idiots who thought of us as their servants, they went around with their noses in the air looking down on us, and some of them were very unkind and occasionally cruel. And then there were the Tidys (Norfolk dialect for good). In the Norfolks we were lucky as there were quite a few of these. Although they were posh, they treated us as professionals, and listened to the experienced voices in the others ranks. They treated us with kindness and respect, so they got our respect in return.

The army talked a lot about leadership, but I thought the real leadership came from the Sergeants and the Sergeant Majors. Many had seen real action in The Boer War. They would tell us stories and we all hoped that one day we would see action, and be able to tell stories of our own. One of the best was Sgt (later CSM and RSM) Charles "Charlie" Aldridge. We reckoned that when the Officers spoke to us, they used lots of long words but said very little. When Charlie spoke, he used a few short words but said a lot. He was strict but had a good old Norfolk sense of humour, combined with huge experience. We believed Charlie cared for us, and that whatever happened, would do his best to look after us. Everyone respected Charlie. The boys followed him willingly. As would be proved over the next ten years, we would do anything for him. Anything.

The Officers told us the history of the regiment and how we were lucky to be joining one of the elite units of the British Army. Apparently the Norfolk's forebears were the 9th Regiment of Foot, established just after Cromwell created his New Model Army in the 17th Century, according to Private "Professor" Williams. The cap badge comes from 200 years ago in 1707 when the 9th Regiment of Foot refused to surrender and covered the defeated army's retreat, and the badge of Britannia was awarded by a grateful Queen Anne. It made us one of the senior units, and as such we would usually be at the spearhead. This meant we would be first in, or held back to be used as a special force, or picked because the job was difficult. Our seniority meant that we were positioned in the "right of the line" in the British Army - a position of huge prestige and importance. We had the greatest empire the world had ever seen. We had the best army. And we, the Norfolk's, were one of the senior units, the best of the best. It made you feel good when you were told this.

The history made its way into our drinking games. My favourite was one called "right of the line". You raise your pint as a toast. It finishes "Right of the line, Pride of the British Army, Terror of the world!" As it goes to each man, you add "A of the B" (such as "Cushion of the Yards") at the front of list, and the list gets longer until one man makes a mistake and then he has to down his drink, and buy the next round. This man was usually my mate Billy, as he got his "ofs" and "offs" confused. If all my days in the army were going to be like my first, I thought to myself, "I'm going to enjoy this". I learnt the importance of humour, and how this would be able to see you through in the army and in life. But for now, I liked the army, and it seemed the army liked me.

2
THE JEWEL OF EMPIRE

… the day Smitty got a Chitty for a Donkey.

Albert in dress uniform (whites) in Belgaum India, 1911.

"They sent us on a great adventure,
The King's business was in hand;
They sent us off to India,
And then the promised land".

After training I joined the First Battalion Norfolk Regiment (1 NORFOLK). Two men were soon to become good friends. Bille and Williams, who we called "Prof" Williams (Professor) on the account that was the cleverest person we had ever met. Both were from Norwich. We had a lot of laughs together on our first posting in Ireland. At the end of one day, and after a long session of "right of the line", Billy, who had gone out for a pee, came rushing into the bar and said, "Have you heard the news? Tomorrow we sail for Belgium to become part of the British Indian Army".

We were all confused. Until "Prof" Williams corrected Billie, saying he had misread it. It was Belgaum not Belgium. Belgaum (now Belagavi) was on the east coast of the sub-continent of India. We were all up for this, particularly as me, Billie and "Prof" were going to transfer together for foreign service, and join the 2nd Battalion.

I spent three happy years in India. On arrival we were photographed in our whites. All the poses were the same and the game became "who could look identical to somebody else in the company". We grew moustaches to help. It was a good job we had the smart whites, as in 1912 the King himself came to Bombay and we were all shipped up to meet him and parade for him. We all had a jolly time.

We got on well with the Indians. I liked them. I found them nice people, in fact very much like us. There were however, some big differences. The Indians did seem more concerned with hierarchy than us, and also a lot more worked up about religion. They seemed to get on better with us than they did with each other, something I always found strange. Units tended to keep themselves to themselves, and we did not do much together other than an occasional game of cricket. But I did have a mate in an Indian Battalion called Mohammed. He was a fast runner which we found out in the cricket games. We called him "Slow-Mo!" I was pretty fast myself, but only over fifty yards, after that the lads with longer legs passed me. The fastest in our company was "Midget". He was six foot two, and built like a gas lamppost. He had a strange running style and we all joked that he could not run in straight line.

Another difference in India, was that everything was paid for by some form of chitty. "Prof" Williams said that chitty came from Hindi meaning "an official note of something that is owed". This could be a bar bill or it could be anything you owed someone else, some clothing, a gift, cigarettes, some food, some cushies (sweets), a favour etc. In my section we had a Private Smith, who was to become my best pal. He was from Pockthorpe (Norwich slum area). He had perfected the art of giving and receiving chitties for almost everything, never paying or getting paid. Sometimes this worked against him, but it usually worked in his favour. Everyone loved him. Private Smith, "Smitty", had an infectious laugh. The lads started to call him "Smitty the Chitty", something he loved. In fact this provided a famous line in the "right of the line" drinking game - but of course it became "Smitty of the Chitty". Smitty would often get this wrong on purpose during the game to increase his status as the company's number one rummun (character). In fact anyone who said Smitty of the Chitty (only to be used in the game) rather than "Smitty the Chitty" (in normal use) was immediately fined, and presented with a chitty!

One day me and Smitty had some jollificearshuns (fun and games) with Slow Mo, whose English was good. We were explaining how you test a Norfolkman. You ask the question, "He'yer fa'got a dickey, bor?" (Has your father got a donkey, boy?). The correct reply is, "Yis, an' he want a fule ter roid 'im, will yew cum?" (Yes and he wants a fool to ride him, will you come?). Smitty and me got into trouble as we encouraged Slow-Mo to ask this question to one of the Twat Officers who was a right P****. He did, and Smitty and me creased up with laughter as "He'yer fa'got a dickey, bor?" was delivered in an Indian accent to the bemused and confused Indian Officer. Our hilarity did not last long, as the Officer immediately put Mo and the two of us on a charge for being insubordinate.

Smitty and I soon ended up in front of our platoon commander, and Mo his. It had the potential to get out of hand but our Officer was a Tidy (a good one), and he thought the whole thing was a joke and wasting his time. He concluded that no one could quite understand who said what to who, and that no one outside the Norfolk can ever speak Norfolk, and the whole thing was dropped and Privates Cushion and Smith were given a stern ticking off and a lecture about respecting culture. Ironic, as Slo-Mo thought the whole thing was brilliant, and was our friend for life. Anyway, our Officer said he had more important things to do than "get wronged" (tell off) with us jokers. We thought it was the game of billiards or cards he had postponed. Actually it turned out he had a staff meeting to be briefed on our next posting ... to Mesopotamia.

When we next saw Mo, we shouted, "Ever heard of Mesopotamia?" Mo laughed, and then said, "Our C/O (Commanding Officer) has told us that Allah created Hell, but it was not bad enough, so he added flies, and called it Mesopotamia". This time we had no idea what he was talking about, but we were soon to find out.

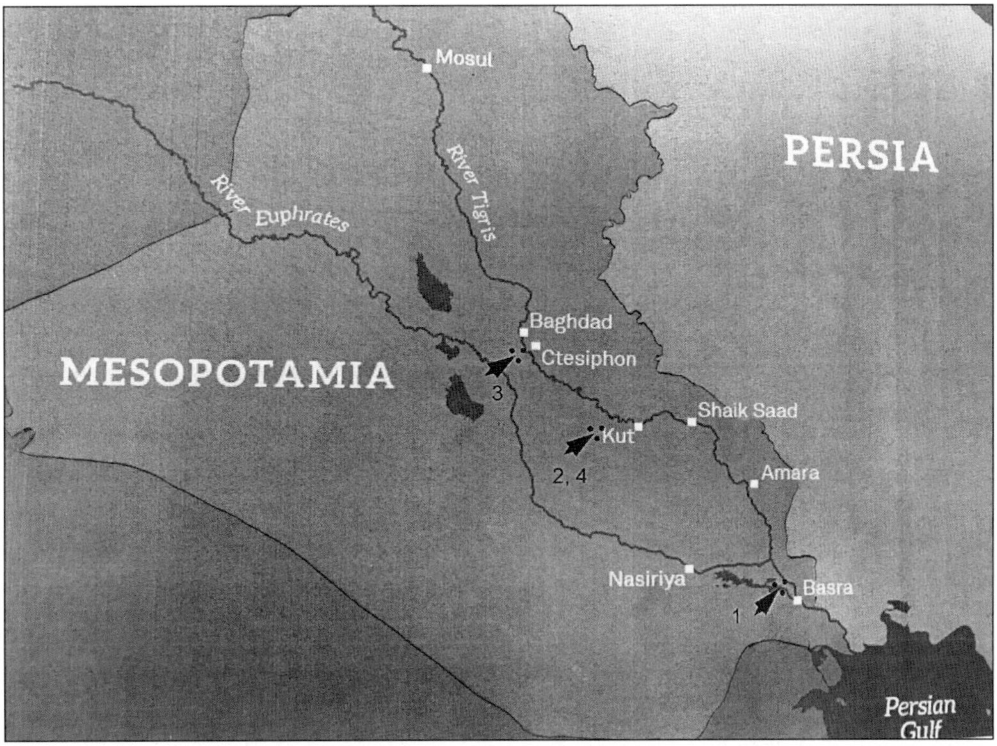

The four great battles of the Tigris Campaign 1914-16:
1. Shaiba, 2. Kut, 3. Ctesiphon, 4. The Siege of Kut.

3

THE 350 YARD DASH IN THE DESERT

... the day Norfolk dashed in the desert - Shaiba day.

Survivors of the The 350 yard dash in the desert.
Picture taken south of Ctesiphon 1915. Albert is second row, kneeling, fifth from the left.

"We ended up in Mesopotamia,
They said we made lots of noise;
They marched us up the Tigris,
They called us the 'holy boys'.

We had heard that things had kicked off in Europe and we were all as "Keen as Colman's" (very keen, keen as Colman's mustard) to get stuck in and do our bit. After five days on the Elephanta (ship), we arrived in Mespot (Mesopotamia) on 11th November 1914. We joined the 7th Rajputs, 110th Mahratta Light Infantry, and the 120th Rajputana Infantry, to form the 18th (Indian) Brigade. Along with the 16th (Indian) Brigade we would form the 6th (Indian) Division. They would all prove to us that they were worthy comrades and fighting men.

Our first action on 17th November was at a place called Shatt-al-Arab, where the rivers Tigris and Euphrates meet. 2 NORFOLK and 7 RAJPUT were spearheading, and with the support of both brigades we soon saw off our new enemy Johnny Turk. After the usual bully beef and tea, we bedded down victorious that night near the old fort, the weather turned and we realised we were short of blankets and greatcoats. Like in India, it was hot, but we were not so used to the cold nights. Along with the Turk sniping, it was not a good night. The boys renamed our location Sh**-al-Arab!

Later in November we jumped aboard SS Madjidieh to go to Basra. There had been a lot of looting and our job there was policing. Basra was pretty dirty with the oil wells smoking by day and burning by night. In December, we moved up to support D Company (2 NORFOLK) and help take the town of Qurna. Apparently this was where the Garden of Eden was meant to be. In reality it was a lot of dirty tracks, and loads of mud-and-reed huts. Most importantly for soldiering, the flooded tracks were too deep to run through and the reeds offered no cover. So we were pretty much exposed every time we moved. We had our first real taste of advancing 100 yards over open ground under heavy fire. We were able to catch Johnny Turk off guard as we attacked swiftly, while the rivers were in full flood.

By the time we got to Mespot I was twenty three years old, and had five years soldiering experience. In my section we had a young lad of eighteen or nineteen, who was new. We were involved in a huge fire fight securing the village of Muzaira, and for the first, and not the last time, we were to fix and clear with bayonets. This lad however was shaking so much that he could not clip his bayonet on. Smithy tried to calm him by saying a bit of "stick and jink" (bayonet technique) would be no worse than a run down Prince of Wales Road (name of notorious road in Norwich) on a Saturday night. This did not really help as the boy had never been down Prince of Wales Road, then Smithy made it worse by admitting neither had he. Spotting the situation, the CSM (Company Sergeant Major) stood up and in full view of the enemy walked slowly over to him. The CSM said, "whas gorn on?" The lad replied with his bayonet shaking in hand and clanking against his rifle fore sights, "I think I'm a bit scared Sergeant Major... are you scared?" To which the CSM replied, standing in full view of the Turk snipers, "NO! They are nothing to be scared of. They're scared of us. But I see you have your boot lace untied, and for that I might put you on a charge! Worry about that, not them". The lad tied his lace and then fixed his bayonet and was ready to go.

Later we developed a skit to calm the nerves of the new boys. We would take old newspapers in our haversacks and while we were waiting we would read them, and when the orders came through we would slowly fold up the newspapers and put them away, before fixing bayonets. This seemed to do the trick. Some of the terrain was bleak, no scenery, no vegetation, and flat. "Flatter than Norfolk" became a term. It was difficult to set your sights (on your rifle) and judge distance and sometimes as we marched, the closer we got to a town or fort the further away they seemed. "Prof" had said this was the mirage effect of the desert.

It was hot. We were told it goes up to "134 degrees in the shade". Which always made us laugh as there never was any shade. We were better prepared for the heat than some, as we had spent so much time in India. For me the heat was not too bad, as you got used to it, but the blessed dust storms which got into your mouth and eyes and other parts, were a real pain. While May to October was hot, November and April were cool, with December to March very cold. In the winter the rain came which turned much of the ground into flooded areas and thick mud. Off duty, we enjoyed the "Smithy's Pontoon School", and although your belt might be bursting with rupees, there was nowhere to spend them. The only luxury was a dip in Tigris if you were lucky enough to be stationed next to it.

Unlike in India, we found the locals a bit shifty. It seemed every time our backs were turned, or we took a village, or the Turks left one, often in a hurry, it would spark a wave of looting and thieving. We all enjoyed the story going round about Lt Spackman who, on his way to the latrine one evening, desperate for a sh**, saw the latrine being carried off by three Arab hoodlums. The boys on guard opened fire. Spackman dived back into his tent. The guard chased the thieves down and got one with the bayonet. Unfortunately in the fire fight, a stray round hit Mr Spackman's tent pole collapsing his tent on top of him with his trousers down. Needless to say this episode made its way into the "Right of the line" game! As well as the phrase, "They'll even steal your sh** if you don't watch out". Not much happened in January 1915 other than dodging enemy artillery, and in February and March we were back in Basra. Then in April, we got the news that we were all hoping for ... we were going on the offensive.

The day I'm going to tell you about is 14th April 1915, which later became Shaiba day. The battle had been rolling for three days with a lot of cavalry action. This day, after a good breakfast, the 18th Brigade advanced in a box square formation with us and 120th in forward positions. Our initial thrust to Old Basra and Zubair proved misguided, so the brigade wheeled round the south mound to Barjisiya Wood. We received a lot of rifle and artillery incoming, in what they call constant fire, a bit short of rapid but going on for hours. We were wet and uncomfortable most of the day, due to the sweat and wading through water, which varied from five inches to five feet. With the heat in its hundreds we were "all of a muckwash" (sweating profusely) so grateful to the bheeties (Indian water carriers), who kept a constant water run going, most of the time under fire. We ended up being pinned down some 350 yards from the Turk positions, which were along about a mile-long ridge. Our C/O reported this and we were told to wait. We were not overly concerned at that point, as we were all pretty knackered.

In an attempt to relieve the pounding we were taking, we were told that we were going to deploy our new secret weapon ... not Smithy's Harry Champion impression, that he claimed was our secret weapon (Harry Champion was a pop star of the day), but the new technology of … aeroplanes. They arrived out of the sun very slowly. When we saw them the boys began to cheer. They looked like giant moths hovering over the sand. As they got near the Turks, they received rifle and artillery fire from the enemy, and they immediately rose up to gain more height. We then saw some packages being dropped from the aeroplanes. "Prof" Williams informed us they were aerial mines (later to be called bombs). Most of them fell into the flooded area, some into no-man's-land, and the few that did fall onto the Turks did not seem to go off. Smithy commented, "Well that was a bloody waste of time, perhaps my Harry Champion impression would have been better". We had to stop Smithy bursting into his rendition of "Boiled beef and carrots", as he was an awful singer. We all concluded that there was probably no future in aerial warfare. We all wanted to have a go at them. Billie asked one of the Officers if we could be next. Something along the lines of, "About time they unleashed the right of the line Sir? The Professionals!" I think the response was something like, "All in good time".

About mid-afternoon we got the news we were waiting for. I was close to Colonel Peebles when the order came through. He got a young staff Officer to read it to him twice. "Push forward at all costs. Take enemy's trench". "Push forward at all costs. Take enemy's trench". The C/O paused for reflection and then moved forward, and ended up standing next to me and Smithy at the front. On his way to us, the young staff Officer who had read the order asked why he was moving to the front of the line, to which the C/O replied, "I cannot lead from the rear!" Few things ever impressed me, but this did. But as I turned to Smithy, I had to stop him doing one of his "rear end and farting" jokes with the Colonel next to us.

Our next order was what we had been waiting for - "Fix Bayonets!" The mood then changed. A bayonet charge is a very loud and aggressive act, usually preceded by an airy silence. The banter dried up, 600+ bayonets all clipped to the end of our Lee-Enfields. Then silence. This is when it gets serious and the fear sets in. Each of us had a different way of dealing with this. Some say nothing. Others pump themselves up. Some hum a tune to distract. Others turn to humour. I was in the last category, probably a way to deal with the fact that your heart is jumping out of your chest, you are fired up, sh** scared, and feeling terrified and physically sick. But this was our job. This was what we were trained to do. And we were bloody good at it.

The silence gave CSM Aldridge the opportunity to do one of his favourite lines, "Well, we have seen the rest, now let's see the best". This always gave me comfort. He was always so good in these situations. I had huge confidence in him. It also dawned on me that it looked like we were all going, the whole battalion, 600+ of us with bayonets fixed. Up to now it had been mainly Company action with an occasional platoon scrap, but this time we would now see what Norfolk could do. Boys from Norwich, Wymondham, Yarmouth, Cromer, all in action together. For a brief moment I thought of home ... The CSM interrupted my thoughts with "Cushion, how far do you think it is?" "About 350 yards Sergeant Major Sir" I replied. Smithy said, "My money is on Cush getting there first". I said, "Don't be silly, I'm only the second fastest in the company, Midget is the fastest. Anyway, it's more than fifty yards, so with my hoddy doddy (very small) legs I won't get there first". But as Smithy pointed out, Midget can't run in a straight line, and he will probably end up in the Flooded Area. We all smiled, but this time nobody laughed.

To understand the next order you need to remember the history of the regiment. Remember we were 2 NORFOLK, descended from the famous 9th Regiment of Foot. The Fighting Ninth. The right of the line, the legend which we had been told about on our first day at Britannia Barracks, five years before. After what seemed like a huge wait the artillery opened up, and this was our cue. We looked at the C/O .... he then drew his sword! Roaring at the top of his voice, "COME ON THE NINTH", he leapt over the ridge. Smithy and me followed him, screaming at the top of our voices, running and firing as fast as we could. A quick glance to left and right was an amazing sight, Norfolk had joined the war. Wow, a battalion bayonet charge, under fire, in 120 degrees, over open ground, with the C/O ahead of us carrying only his sword. You don't see that very often. Then it started, rata-tata-tata-tata-tata, but you don't really hear it with the screaming, firing and exploding shells.

We got to what seemed about halfway when something extraordinary happened. The machine gun fire stopped and the Turks started to leg-it from their positions. The screaming on our side turned to cheering. I was relieved because trench clearing with a bayonet is not the most pleasant part of soldiering. Looking back, seeing Norfolk running at you, screaming with bayonets fixed, must have been an amazing and frightening sight for them. The Turks turning and running was something, unfortunately for us, that was not to happen often. Johnny Turk was usually a formidable, skilled and highly determined foe.

Once I had cleared the wire, I dropped onto the waddi (dry river bed), previously held by the Turks. To my amazement Smithy was already there. He was sitting down, smoking, with his bayonet embedded in the sand. He said, "You took your time. I've been here for bloody hours". And then declared, "Smitty of the Chitty, claims this 'Shitty' land of Shaiba, for Norwich and our City". Although I was still gasping for breath, I roared with laughter, and so did he.

And then, like being hit by a hurricane from nowhere, we were joined in the trench. It was CSM Aldridge. "What the F*** is going on here? Get to your F****** feet, F****** fix that F****** bayonet Smith. If I had been a F****** Turk both of you F****** jokers would be F****** dead". He was not pleased. Unlike some CSMs he did not swear often so we knew this time he was annoyed. Smithy leapt to his feet, "Yes Sergeant Major". Seeing his words had the desired effect, the CSM calmed down. Maybe feeling he had been a bit unfair on me, as he passed me he said, "At least Cushion is on his feet with bayonet fixed, and looks like a F****** soldier". He then disappeared. Knowing he was right, and feeling like two told off school boys, but mainly seeing who could get the last laugh in, I lunged forward as though I was heading a football, saying "Cushion scores at the Nest, ONE-ONE! Smitty-might-have-a-chitty but it's Cushion who scores-for-City!" We both burst out laughing again. This was a bloody good day soldiering.

4

THE "BLOODY NOSE" AT CTESIPHON

... the day it started to go wrong.

A rare moment where the "Comfortable" Commissariat Carts were not carrying the wounded. Near Ctesiphon. Mesopotamia, 1915.

"They said we fought very well,
They said we couldn't be beaten;
But then we got a bloody nose,
Our concern was what we'd eaten!"

We had quite a lot wounded so we fell back to Basra. In the sweltering heat of June and July, there were lots of small actions. Johnny Turk seemed to have stiffened his resolve and put up more of a fight in each than we were expecting. In September we moved them out of a place called Kut and we halted at Ali-al-Gharbi.

Supplies were low also due to low river levels making resupply a problem. I remember this period as one of high sickness. The food was completely S**** and many of the lads had come down with Beriberi. At one point we had over 50 of the battalion who should have been in hospital being treated in the field. On the grape vine there was a lot of discussion as to the wisdom of pushing on to Baghdad. In November we were to go on the offensive again, to a place called Ctesiphon (pronounced with a silent C). Smithy and I had great fun with the name of this place. While we all struggled to pronounce it, one of the Officers of the Dorset's had a lisp and stutter, and could not say it right. It was hilarious. It should be TES-I-FON. He came up with, or at least we said he said, CEST-I-FON, KEST-I-FON, QUESTI-FON, INSIST-UPON, INCEST-UPON, AND PEST-I-FON. My favourite was Smithy's PIST-A-PON. Given the sickness in the camp and the grumbling about the equipment and medical supplies this seemed most appropriate. It soon spread across the battalion and became THE accepted description.

Smithy and I turned this into an exam we would give any of the Dorset's we met. Your Mesopot field test is to pronounce the following: Ctesiphon, Happisburgh, Great Hautbois, and Wymondham. Easy for a Norfolkman, impossible for anyone else. These games helped us when we were marching. Another one was we will "hetter keep a dewun" (no alternative but to keep going), which we would put about while waiting for the next order, which would usually be to advance. But this sky larking about (messing about), hid the general poor conditions we were existing under. While Shaiba had all gone our way, at Ctesiphon everything seemed against us.

The day I want to tell you about was not a good one for me or the battalion. It made Shaiba look like a picnic. When the dead, wounded and sick were totally up, we were at less than half-strength. This was the official version from the Officers. Unofficially it was worse. Most of us who were classified as fit, myself included, were actually sick. Some of us did not report that we were sick, and others who did were told they were fit. "Got a bit of jip" (pain) became the normal description for anything short of being unable to fight. No Norfolkman would ever declare himself unable to fight.

A fierce battle took place within the sight of The Great Arch of Ctesiphon. The gun fire and battle noise seemed to bounce off and be amplified by The Great Arch in a sinister way; throwing the sound into the desert like a great banjo resonator. I remember arriving at the end of action at the RV (Rendez Vous or meeting point), knackered, sick and parched as usual. The Platoon Sergeant was doing the roll call. I answered my name and then switched off… until he got to Smith … there was a silence … he spoke under his breath as he marked his note pad with his pencil, "MISSING".

Missing? Smithy? Missing? Impossible! I can't remember if I spoke this out, or said it to myself in my head, but I reacted. I can't explain how I felt. I think I was in shock. The Sergeant looked at me and said "Cushion, stand firm, we have a job to do". My mind was racing. Losing men was part of the job but I never thought it would be Smithy. Initially I refused to accept it, but by nightfall it had been confirmed. We had lost Smithy.

Things for me would not be the same again. Smithy had become my best mate in our band of brothers. If you have ever served in uniform you will know what I mean. If you have not, I can't explain it. We were a good pair, the pair of jokers as the CSM called us. I was disciplined, ordered, punctual, diligent, quiet and sensible. Smithy was the opposite. He was scruffy, got lots of things wrong, a walking disaster area, "fumble fisted" (clumsey) and carefree. We shared a great sense of humour. A Norfolk sense of humour. If you have ever been in a tight spot, you will know how important it is to keep up morale. Smithy was the king of this. I would miss him. We were told we were the best. Smithy for me was the best of the best. Above all he had something, probably the most important quality in professional soldering. All the Norfolks had it, but Smithy had it more than the rest of us. He believed he could never be beaten. He would crack on, march on, or fight on, regardless of the situation. The worse it got, the stronger his belief. Smith had undefeatable spirit.

5

THE ORDER: HOLD FOR A MONTH

... Mo's day. One in the five months of the Siege of Kut-Al-Amara
(the longest siege in British military history).

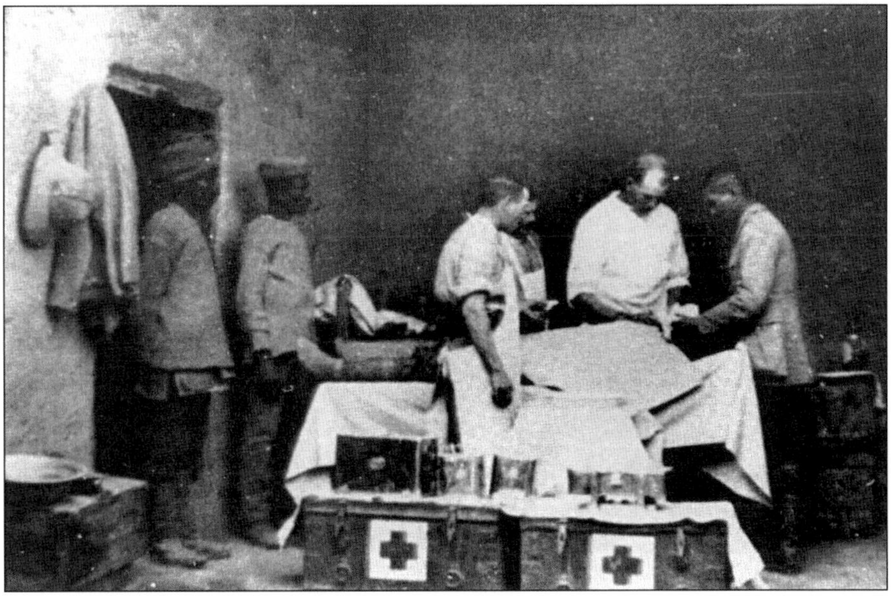

The hospital at Kut-Al-Amara, 1916.

"They ordered us to fall back, and hold a place call Kut;
They promised to relieve us, some doubted that they would.
They surrounded us, and besieged us, would we stay alive?
'Hold for one month', we held on for five.
They starved us, and only horse, less and less until ...
All too weak to stand, and most of us were ill."

After marching and retiring over 44 miles within 36 hours, we eventually arrived exhausted at the river bend town we were to defend. Until now Basra had been the foulest place we had ever visited, but the boys said that this place made Basra seem like Yarmouth in comparison. It was called Kut (Kut-al-Amara), which we had battled earlier to take. Kut was a hot, oppressive and generally a stinking place.

Our first job, the first week of December, was to deal with mass looting. Once we had settled in, not much happened for the rest of the month, apart from the daily attacks from enemy aeroplanes. One of the Norfolk Officers had a gramophone. And most nights we would hear it blasting out the musical hall song, "Get out and get under (the automobile)". We knew all the words and found this entertaining and funny, well it was for the first hundred times anyway. We would get stick from the CORNWALL's on attachment with us, particularly my mate "Paddy" Kearney, who would shout when he heard it, "When are the Norfolk's going to fix that blessed car?" To which our reply was often something like, "It got damaged on the dodgy roads in Cornwall!" The CORNWALLs were up in advanced positions around the fort, and I agreed with Paddy he should take the gramophone up to his position and play this song all Christmas day to the Turks, which would probably cause their surrender. This was stopped by the fact that the Officer was not keen on letting it go forward, and after the Christmas present of the bombardment the Turks sent us, all the forward positions were a wreck.

It was not long before we had more outbreaks of disease on our hands to deal with as well. In the first few weeks the Turks increased their efforts around us, blockading the river and digging-in around the town. We were surrounded and it was soon the Officers were using the term "Siege".

Apparently they had sent the message to London, and India, that we needed to be relieved and a relief column was coming. According to our C/O the Generals had told London we had one months' worth of food, but he reckoned we had enough for two. I think the idea was to get the bureaucrats and bunglers in London moving. Then the order came through, "Hold for a month". Not a pleasant place to stay, but most of us thought a few weeks would be doable. The nights were cold and we lived-in-boots in the trenches for weeks, but we all hoped for the relief column to get through soon, as it had done at Ladysmith and Chitral. In fact the Officers found time to celebrate the anniversary of the relief of Ladysmith. Billy was detailed to help out and he showed me the menu, and someone had had a good laugh with it. I remember "Windy Lizzy Pudding, with Flatulent Fanny Sauce" as the sweet.

In the winter months, since Ctesiphon, I had grown a bit in confidence and partly taken on Smithy's role leading the comedy in the company. It seemed the more desperate the situation, the more we needed it. I was enjoying this new role. One piece of good news for the Battalion was that CSM Aldridge was made RSM (Regimental Sergeant Major). Good news for everyone. Although it did mean we did not see him as much each day.

In January rations were cut to half, and then cut again in February. In February the all-out assaults had stopped but it turned to sniping and shelling, plus those mines from aeroplanes. The latter did not prove much of a threat to us because you would hear them coming and take cover early. The artillery Officers would also warn us when the aeroplanes were on the way, often as the sun was falling. "Here comes Fritz, take cover", was the order, on account of the fact that the aeroplanes were German, flown by the Germans allied to the Turks. While not much of a bother to us, they hit the hospital and buildings with civilians. They mainly targeted these buildings and we were in the trenches. One of our Officers told me that the General had called this "cowardly barbarism worthy of Chinese pirates". We dreaded getting a Blighty (serious wound requiring patient to be shipped back to Britain), as this meant being sent to hospital and due to the air attacks, this seemed a more dangerous place than in the trench. Dysentery and scurvy were rife but the most notable thing was that at this time we ran out of tea. Some of the boys improvised with dried leaves, sawdust and ginger, and so called "ginger water". The Sepoys found a way of harvesting grass, so called "sag". Basically wet hay, and when doused in vinegar some of the boys said it was not too bad, but I could never take to it. A big day was when the ciggies ran out, but at least we lost less men from sniping, under the three light rule. The first light he sees you, second light he sets his sights, third light he fires. So we shared a match with only one other chum.

The siege was to go on for five months not one. As we entered March and April rations were cut further to starvation rations. We had a couple of months of plenty, then a couple of months of adequate rations, which reduced over time, and then the last month was starvation rations. It ended up 3oz of bread, and 1 ½ oz of horse/mule a day per man. When the salt ran out, the meat tasted worse. Occasionally someone would catch a mud fish from the Tigris. This looked awful, smelt awful and tasted worse, but we were grateful for anything. We were hungry all the time. Dysentery grew. Our aeroplanes tried to drop food, but they were as successful as their first time. Some packages missed, some ended up behind Turk lines and some disintegrated on impact. I suppose at least they tried.

We would get regular communiqués from the General, which we valued, and I remember one that ended with "Save your ammunition as if it is gold". With the communiqués, the estimates of food stocks seemed to change a lot, in fact, every time they counted them. I overheard a discussion amongst some of the Sergeants, in "Sergeants mess ginger water brew up", where they agreed that we appeared to have plenty of ammunition, which we were not using much, but very little food, which were using up fast. But they concluded that the General must know what he is doing. Interestingly we interpreted the communiqués as "opeful bucks" (well intentioned hopeful desires/wants), but the Sepoys took these communiqués as cast iron truths or promises and therefore seemed more effected when the bad news of the unsuccessful RF (Relief Force) efforts came through.

Unlike our Officers in 2 NORFOLK we never saw much of the General in person, although our Officers said he was approachable, and "Charlie" or "Alfonse" as they called him, would spend time with them. At the time, most of us liked and respected General Townsend. He had led us to capture a lot of ground and win some notable victories with limited battlefield casualties. He, like us, preferred to be on the offensive. So by these measures he was good.

Infantry soldiers like a winner who is mindful of the cost, and as things had gone our way, "Townsends luck" became a term, which they said he liked, being a student of Napoleon and military history. Apparently he also played the banjo, something which the musical lads liked. However, there was also a rumour that he spent most of his time sucking up to the "important people" and entertaining them for tea and tiffin, hence his nickname, "Tiffin Townsend". Anyway, that's how we felt at the time. After the war when we heard some of the treacherous and disgraceful things he had said and done later, and the lies he said about us, opinions towards him hardened. His nickname changed, but that's another story.

We did see more of the General's dog called Spot. We played "spot the dog" with the winner getting ciggies. With all the field promotions and maybe due to the General's profile, it was rumoured that the dog had been promoted to a General, and the game renamed to "Spot the General". Billie reckoned he came up with this. "Prof" Williams said that it was indeed a fine joke, but was too clever for Billie to have invented so was probably something that the DORSET'S had invented. This annoyed Billie as he was adamant it was his gag. This also annoyed Boggis, the General's batman who was also a Norfolkman, and had worked at Raynham Hall (The Townsend family Norfolk Estate and seat) before he signed up.

All of us seemed to fall into one of three categories: the starving, the ill, or the starving and ill. Our clothes became ragged, as we shrank sizes inside them, and washing them and personal ablutions became a problem. As Spring came and the bad weather dried up, the lice arrived, and typhus broke out. The RSM (Regimental Sergeant Major) decided to step up drill practice and this had the effect of raising morale. As professionals we knew if we could drill, we could fight, and it boosted our confidence to show to each other and ourselves that we could still do it. Despite our situation, morale was good. Well it was in the Norfolks. After all we had every reason to be confident. We had chased the Turks all the way up the Tigris close to Baghdad, advanced over huge territory and in the main with limited battlefield casualties. We had proved that we were a match and better for anything they had. On our side, it was said that the

Mohammedans would not be too keen to fight the Turks, especially given the sacred places we were fighting in. My experience was however, that they could be relied upon. The Indians fought well and were good soldiers.

But through lack of food, we were all slowing dying. This was not helped by D Forces' (name of the expeditionary force) lack of medical equipment and supplies which had plagued us since we landed in Mespot. We created a "bone roll", about one in five portions of horse had a bone and this was a bit tastier, so we took it turns to have this. When you are short of food it tends to dominate your existence. You dream of it and are constantly searching around for it. I mainly craved bread. The Indian boys had it the worst. Some of them refused to eat horse on religious grounds. While we respected this, we could not really understand it. At one point we were losing fifteen of them a day. Some continued this refusal despite a dispensation from the Iman. In some units the non-Muslims got reduced rations to give this to the Muslims in lieu of meat and this caused some grumbling. Each morning at "Stand To" we would hear the Muezzin call the faithful to prayer, and this would drift across no-man's-land; in a strange and ironic way this uplifting beautiful spiritual voice would be the signal for the killing to begin.

The day I am going to talk about is the one when I had heard that my friend Mo, of cricket fame, was dying of starvation and was one of the guys refusing to eat. I popped over to his unit to check on him and found him in the sick bay. "Hi Cush" he said as I entered the building. I opened with, "Hi Mo, rumour is that you are going on a diet to lose weight to make your cricket fielding faster". He smiled. I continued, "Now I've brought you some meat and you need to eat it". "I can't" he said. "Why not?" I enquired. "You know I can't eat the meat due to religion" said Mo. "That's crazy" I said. "You need to eat, and on the menu at restaurant Kut there is only meat". Mo, "But my religion bans me from eating meat". I was now getting cross, "F*** religion," I said.

It went quiet. I realised I might have overstepped the mark. He then came back with, "What and who are we fighting for? We are fighting for the British Empire and British Values – Yes?". "Yes" I agreed. "And don't you British believe that a man should be free to choose his religion and that whatever he chooses, that should be respected?" "Yes", I had to agree again. He continued, "Then I choose Islam and you should respect that". I realised I was losing, and I became more heated. I continued, "Look Mo, if you don't eat you will die. I DO respect your religion but I'm here as your friend, I don't want you to die". Mo then concluded, "Whether I die or not, is not in your hands or mine, it's in the hands of Allah".

I realised I had got as far as we were going to get. The truth is, I could not think of a witty reply without disrespecting him, so I said nothing. I wished him well and retired back to base. I really felt S*** on the walk back. What sort of religion made a good man die? But then should I have tried to stop a man following his faith? Had I done enough for a friend? Overall I felt I had given a pretty poor account of myself. I wondered if Smithy had been with us, would we have been more successful? I doubted it. After some guard duties at the Serai (billet), I went back that night to check on him again. On entering the sick bay, I discovered he was no longer there. Mo had passed away.

6
THE SURRENDER: DAY 147

... the day we surrendered, 29th April 1916.

The Indian boys had it worse, Kut, April 1916.

"The Indian boys had it worse, as they could not eat horse;
Don't worry lads, a few more days, 'Stiff upper lip' of course.
Day 147. They said we had to surrender, is this what the British Army do?
When they ordered 'destroy all arms', most of us, were on the loo!
With relief just miles away, they said they saw our smoke;
We kept the humour going, the lads love a joke.
But while we were laughing, the relief O/C cried;
We knew, like us, they'd done their best, at least they had tried."

Towards the end of March the rains came, and with the rising Tigris, substantial flooding followed. Both us and the Turks had to abandon some trenches as they were water clogged. This had the benefit of reducing the sniping, but this annoyance was replaced by another, a swarm of flies and a plague of hopp'n toads (frogs). Not a good omen according to some of our CofE (Church of England) boys. The toads ate the flies and then became too fat to jump out of the trenches. We spent most of the days cutting steps for the toads to get out of the dugouts, so we didn't have to stand or lie on a bed of hopp'n toads.

As March passed we were getting weaker and weaker. We would often hear the "boom, boom, boom" of the RF (Relief Force) guns. British RFs usually got through, so we were optimistic. One day they were very loud, maybe less than ten miles ways. The RSM brought us to Stand To. Energy levels soared as we got ready for a break-out. We expected that we would be asked to be the "tip of the spear" (lead unit). Most of us would have been much happier trying to fight our way out, than sit there and starve. As Billie said, "If we are going to go, let's go together fighting, rather than on our own, drowning in our own s***." We were conscious of the sacrifices of the boys who were trying to break through and relieve us, and we wanted to help them. We might be able to take some pressure off the RF. Most of the lads calculated that causalities for us would be high, but no worse than what we were experiencing by holding fast. It became the most frequent request that we asked the RSM to pass on to the Officers. Sitting and doing nothing is not something we were good at or liked. Later that day the guns faded, and we were told to Stand Down. Morale dipped as at this point as we realised that it was likely that the break-out option was now not on the cards. In a later communiqué from the General, another failed attempt of the RF had been confirmed.

The day finally came when it was difficult for us to mount the guard, due to the fact most of us were too weak to stand up. The word quickly spread that we were going to surrender. Billie told the RSM that we should continue, and that we should fight-on, and we could "still shoot the buggers sitting down if necessary". The RSM replied that he had already suggested this to the C/O (Commanding

Officer), and that the C/O had passed this to the General. The General had said that our spirit was commendable and along with the Oxfords and the Dorsets, the Norfolks had always been his "sheet anchor", but an army needs to be able to manoeuvre and if it cannot stand, he had no army. We reluctantly came to terms with the reality of where we were.

Then came the order to "destroy all arms". Now we knew there was no going back. This was the first time I had seen some of the experienced lads cry. The springs in our rifles and bolts were tossed into the river, the rifles buts broken or burnt. Most of us did this in the usual efficient Norfolk way, but some of the lads threw their rifles into the fire loaded and the ammunition went off. The RSM went mad, and they got a B*********! He said, and we had heard this many times before, "There are many ways to do this, and then there is the right way. We are NORFOLKs. We do it the right way".

The thing is, we had never surrendered before so no one knew what to expect. I saw the Union Jack come down, it was faded, shot to pieces, ravaged by bullets, shrapnel and the storms of the desert, but still recognisable and defiant. A bit like us. It was neatly folded by two of us and taken to the General. It was replaced by a white hospital sheet, which stood out against the grey of the morning sky.

It must have been an extraordinary sight for the Turks who came in well-armed and well fed to be met by skeletons in ragged clothes hardly able to stand up. As the Turks entered Kut I remember the RSM ordering every man to his feet, telling us that we had surrendered but we had not been beaten. He pointed out that while we had taken their position many times, they had never once taken ours. We were surrendering because we had run out of food, not because they had beaten us. I asked the RSM what we should do when they arrived. He said, "Get to your feet Cushion, and look 'em in the eye". I did. Word spread. And then I looked around. Every Norfolkman was on his feet, the sick, the ill, the dying. Norfolk had stood up. We had all looked them in the eye. I had never felt prouder. Surrendered but not beaten.

The first Turk unit in looked disciplined and well ordered. I could see they seemed shocked at our condition. This unit treated us well. Later units were less disciplined and it was not long before wrist watches, boots and other kit were being nicked and a lawless state fell over the garrison. So far this was one of the worst days for all of us. One of our Officers told us that he had been informed that we would all be now "The honoured guests of the Sultan". We would soon find out what this meant. I had survived dysentery, cholera, plague, typhus, beriberi, sand-fly, malaria, heatstroke, scurvy, sniping, shooting, bombing, starvation, and now surrender. I did not think things could get much worse, but then they did.

7
THE 1000 MILE DEATH MARCH

... the day we started the march through hell – honoured guests of the Sultan.

The march from Kut, April 1916.

"They said it's worse than Yorktown, would our action be misunderstood?
Only three-in-ten would make it through, we did the best we could.
They said we were their prisoners, to us they were not kind;
They forced us on a death march, the fight was in our mind.
They stole from us, stoned us, starved us, killed the sick, when we fell;
Made us march 1000 miles, to a desert hell."

We were to discover that like us, the Turks were a mixed bag. Some were good soldiers and some were not. And some were nasty B*******. To be fair, I don't think they quite knew what to do with us all, and given our health, I think we were a big problem for them. We learnt later that by day 146, 70% of the garrison had fallen, so those of us left were the three in ten. We also learnt that there had been some high level wheeling and dealing. The Turks wanted petrol in exchange for our safe passage. The British High Command said they do not do deals, and we should be treated as prisoners of war. They then sent a chap called Lawrence (of Arabia), who apparently offered to pay them a lot of money for our safe passage, which annoyed the Turks who said they don't do deals! The end result was the usual ... the higher ups and Toffs all fell out, and left us blokes in the S***.

The Officers were separated from us quickly and whisked off to who knows where. The Colonel and the other Norfolk Officers made time to say goodbye and wish us well. It was usual practice then for Officers and other ranks to be separated, but you could see some of the Officers were not happy leaving us. We had been through so much together. The Colonel said we were in for a long march, but if anyone could march their way home, the Norfolks could. He said, "Remember who we are", and then turning to RSM, and still speaking to us but looking him in the eye said, "You are in good hands". Finally, "Carry on Sergeant Major". They saluted each other, and the Officers left.

I don't know whether the Turks were mad about the wheeling and dealing or just hated us. They treated us badly. The strange thing to us was that the Turk Officers treated their own soldiers badly as well. It made the worst British Officers look like angels. We had found another "T" for our classification of Officers. Some of the Muslim Indians got better treatment and you could see they were trying to get them to turn and fight for them, as fellow Muslims, with the offer of freedom and food etc. The Turks started by looting and thieving and then they executed the local Arabs in Kut, who they said were collaborators. This annoyed us, as we had got on well with the Arabs and they did not deserve this. After all, both us and the Turks were actually guests in their country.

With virtually no food, and no water, and poor kit, mainly starving, mostly ill, S****** ourselves with dysentery, and no transport, they decided to march us through the desert. It was pretty rough. On the first day our rations were two handfuls of wheat. There was no fire wood to burn it, so we soaked it and tried to eat it raw. They gave us biscuits but we soon found that they would swell in your stomach and some lads died from the swelling, so I decided to nibble mine slowly.

They stole our boots and possessions, kicked, punched and flogged the lads, and worse. Soon out of Kut we were marched through some of the local towns where we had been policing. The Arabs would draw their knives across their throats, shout "English finish" and spit at us. Some were invited by the Turks to stone us. Some did. The first stage of the march was 100 miles to Baghdad. At one point we went two days without water. Your throat swells, your lips turn black and you can't talk. We had no means to carry water so we had to march on until we came to a wadi, river or oasis. When we did find it, it often put typhoid germs into our stomachs; some of the boys could not accept the huge amount of water they consumed at once, and this killed them. In the first few days Billy screamed at them when he ran out of water. Some angry Turks grabbed him and forced down him a few pints, until he went unconscious. Then he died.

When our boys fell, often from a rifle butt in the back, we did our best to help them up. If we didn't do this, they would be left behind. Sometimes we were bayoneted when we fell and left. You were not allowed to fall-out, even to relieve yourself. If you did, you were beaten. We came to dread the shouts of "Yallah Yallah" (hurry up). There were a few carts and we were able to use these to carry the dead or those too ill to walk. If we lost a man we did our best to look after the body and bury him properly at day's end. Sometimes the Turks or Arabs would loot these graves for spare blankets. Some of us traded clothing for food. This increased when it became clear that at night, the Arabs would steal all we had. Relieving yourself at night was a problem since you might be ambushed, stripped and beaten. We reverted to going naked to avoid this. There were no roll calls or records kept by the Turks, we were told we were not PoWs (Prisoners of War).

The RSM did his best to monitor who was alive, who was ill and who was dead.

After a few days in Baghdad we were paraded and if you could not stand, you were left there. And I've no idea what happened to these lads. I could stand, so marched on, for what turned out to be another 900 miles. There were hundreds of rag-tag units of prisoners all making their way north, into Syria and Turkey. The towns and cities became stations for the sick and lost prisoners, dirty, hot, noisy, complete chaos, with food being sold to anyone who had anything they could exchange or barter. We met a few Germans who were kind to us. Like us they were professional soldiers and were shocked at the way we had been mistreated and neglected. They ordered the Turks to get us out of the sun. When we got to Mosul they segregated the Hindus and Sikhs from the British and Muslim Indians. The Hindu and Sikh Indians, and the Ghurkhas, had it even worse than us, as they were treated as sub human. Other things happened that I am not going to talk about.

After weeks of desert marching, parched, sick and heat stroke in the day, robbed, beaten and abused at night, we eventually arrived at our destination, in Turkey. We had marched over 1000 miles from Kut. This would be where we would meet some new friends, the Ausees (Australians), who were a great laugh. They had been fighting somewhere we had never heard of called Gallipoli. But then again, they had never heard of Kut. We were to see out the last two years of the war as slave labour, building a railway, in something they called a concentration camp. Only three in ten of those of us who surrendered at Kut survived the march and camp. With only three in ten surviving the siege, it meant that by 1918, of the original 1200 Norfolks there were only 120 left to board the boat home. One in ten.

Days would blur into one. But for the one in ten, one man had kept us all going. At the end of many of these days he would say, "Remember who we are". We did.

8
THE CAMP

… the days we do not talk about.

"They made us build a railway, concentration camp ... 2-year,
Had we been forgotten? Did anybody care?
In 1918. They said it was all over, they said it's now all done;
They said they could not break us, and told us that we'd won.
The 2nds mustered at the boat, the RSM, had a pen;
Of battalion strength that disembarked, we now had one-in-ten."

9
THE MARCH HOME

… the day we marched back into Britannia Barracks.

Britannia Barracks, unchanged, but home had.

"They called it 'war to end all wars', they said it was now all done;
And then they discharged us, no need for your gun.
But home had changed and so had we, there was no time to be kind;
We looked around the Norfolk homes, not the ones we left behind."

The train arrived back at Thorpe Station in my home city of Norwich about mid-afternoon. Trucks were waiting to take us to Britannia Barracks on the hill above the City. I don't know why, as the army was quite happy to let us march thousands of miles when we were in the field, now we were home, they have to send vehicles for the one and a half miles to barracks. That's the army, and you don't ask why.

When we got to the bottom of Kett's Hill, the trucks pulled over. I then heard a voice I recognised. It was RSM Charlie Aldridge, "2 NORFOLK disembark here". I leapt out of the lorry leaving the other boys who we had shared the train with, still in the vehicles bemused. Great, this would be one of Charlie's ruses. I noted that the regimental band had formed up on the other side of the road.

I then said to the RSM, "What's goin' on Sergeant Major Sir?" Charlie said in a voice that only Sergeant Majors can do, "The rest are going to ride home, as for the best, we are going to march home!" It sent shivers down my neck. Then he turned to me, "Too many questions Cushion, now shut up and form up". I smiled and I thought to myself, this is the way to come home.

Then there was a bit of a commotion and squit (nonsense) going on ahead. Apparently some Officer none of us had ever met, had assumed he would be leading us home. He was disabused of this mistake when one of the Platoon Sergeants told him that unless he was at Kut he should F*** O**, and let Charlie lead us home. Someone shouted that he doubted the Officer could even spell Kut. I had to explain to a bloke in the truck that the joke was that a letter might be missing. According to later accounts, some of the boys had told the Officer they were not moving unless the RSM gave the order. The Officer threatened to put them on charge. Eventually the RSM had to go and have chat with the Officer and defuse the situation. The Officer stood aside and Charlie stepped up. Charlie later told us he advised the Officer not to be too harsh with us, since we were all a bit mad having been in the desert for so long and that 2 NORFOLK marched at one speed, which was "sprinting", usually with bayonets fixed, so anyone in front of us was likely to get bayoneted, Officers included, and he did not want the Officer to come to any harm.

The RSM took up position and you could hear a pin drop. He was then to give his final ever order to us. There were 120 of us coming home, barely enough to form a scratch company, not the 1200 of the Battalion of 2 NORFOLK who marched out of the barracks in 1909 ten years earlier. Now one in ten coming home. Charlie looking serious said, "Now you lot. Listen in. Remember who WE are. And remember this time, THEY are watching".

I looked around and could see no one watching, just a woman with a perambulator (pram) looking quizzically at us from across the street. Then it dawned on me who THEY were ... the Battalion, the other 1000. There was a pause. Charlie continued ...

"As THEY will be watching us, god help you if you don't keep step and look F****** sharp. We march home at full strength". Charlie always chose his words carefully and every man knew the significance of the order. He knew and we knew, there was no need for him to advise us on our drill, but it added to the drama of the occasion. Our drill that day, was as ever, punctiliously correct. He continued, "BATALLION. Battalion will march home by column in threes, by the left, quick march".

As we stepped off, the band started to play Rule Britannia. The tradition had always been to march home, up Mousehold Hill to the band playing Rule Britannia. This was the right way to come home, the Norfolk way. At first I felt great pride. Not only had we done our best, we had proved to the world that we were the best. We were 2 NORFOLK, the right of the line, the pride of the British Army. But as we climbed Mousehold Hill my emotions changed. I thought about the other boys; Smithy, Billie, Midget, Prof Williams, Mo and the others, who were still in the desert. We had left the 'best of the best' in the desert. I then felt very sad, then guilty. Very guilty. And then angry. So angry I wanted to punch someone in the face. But I had learnt in the desert, to survive, to control my emotions. They were not helpful, so I locked them away, and just focused on the music and marched on.

So it was with a chest full of pride that I re-entered the main gate of Britannia Barracks, ten years after I had left. Everything about it looked the same. We were finally home. But as we wheeled round the parade ground for the last time, I was hit with another wave of sadness. It dawned on me that my great adventure was nearly at an end. After we were dismissed they gave us a mug of tea and some food and then we each had a de-brief with an Officer. I think I got a Tidy. I went through our journey of ten years, from Britannia through Bombay, Basra, Shaiba Bayonet Charge, Ctesiphon Bloody Nose, the Siege of Kut, Starvation, Surrender, the 1000 mile death march and the camp. I could see he was amazed, impressed and shocked. At the end of my story, he put his pencil down and said, "Bet you would not want to go back there again in a hurry?" A stupid question I thought. And for some reason it made me even more annoyed. He had no idea what we had been through. No one could, unless you were there. And then I blurted out rather angrily, "Yes we would go back. We are 2 NORFOLK, all good soldiers and all good men, we'd go back if we had to".

I'm not sure why I was angry, but I was. And with my blood boiling and still feeling he needed both barrels I added ... "But not without Charlie ... I mean RSM Aldridge ... Charlie cared for us ... Charlie got us home! We'd go back, but not without him". The Officer picked up his pencil again and paused. "I don't know, Private Cushion, because I was not there. A fellow cannot know unless he was there. But I think you might have defined a rare thing, that many talk about, but few experience, something that is beyond praise. It's called Leadership".

10

THE MARCH BACK TO THE YARDS

… the day we never came home.

Not at home: Bertie Cecil, Albert's Brother.
A Territorial who volunteered for Foreign Service with 1/4 Norfolks.
Died in Gallipoli, 1915.

"They said we were a 'band of brothers', but Bertie is not here.
They told us to forget it, did they really care?
They said it's time to move on, no more marching now you're home;
Our hardest fight was yet to come, this time we marched alone."

Dressed in my demob suit, I made my way to the gate to leave Britannia Barracks for the last time. To my delight RSM Aldridge was there to shake my hand and wish me well. Unlike most of us, he was staying in the army. I said, "Are they so short of people they are keeping you in?" We both laughed. He came back with, "They are not short of people but they are keeping the short people", Charlie being five foot four and a half inches like me. The RSM went on with a smile, "You'll never guess Cush, the War Office wallahs sent my mum a telegram saying I was dead!" "Are you?" I said… "Apparently not" he said, "They told her I was dead and then she got one of those postcards we sent from Kara Pisser (Afion Kara Hisser, Concentration Camp, Turkey). They sent a second telegram to her which read 'It is considered that there can be no doubt that the report that RSM Aldridge is dead was a mistake.'" I then added "Blimey, getting again (born again), dead, and now risen. Well, in the desert some of the Holy Boys always thought you were Jesus Christ, now you have proved it". We laughed again. Then he looked me in the eye and said, "Dew you keep you a marchin' Cush!" (from dew you keep a troshin, meaning carry on, goodbye, take care of yourself). I looked him in the eye, and initially there was silence. After all we had been through together, neither of us knew what to say at this point. I broke the tension with, "Got to dash". He added, "Hopefully you will dash a bit quicker than when you were in the desert, and get there first this time". We laughed again and then I set off home.

The walk to Pyes Yard took me just 15 minutes, down Mousehold Hill and along by the river. Familiar places that I had not seen for 10 years. When I got back home, it was good to see my dad again. He seemed pleased to see me and so was my step mum. Within seconds I had sat down, my step mum had rustled up some tea, and as she gave me the mug I looked up at her and said, "Where's Bertie"? There was silence. My dad then said quietly, "A place called Gallipoli". I knew what this meant. The Aussies in the camp had told me, and it sounded like an even bigger cock-up than Kut. There was silence again for what seemed like minutes. I knew when I joined up that I might be in danger but never dreamed that Bertie would not make it. No one said anything. What could you say?

My dad asked me what I was going to do now. I said I had no idea. He informed me that I had better move fast as he thought jobs would be scarce. He was a boot maker and had a job at the factory at St Marys. "You need to know Albert, that the girls did a good job in the factory while you were away and with all the lads coming back from the war, there won't be enough work for everyone. Particularly, now we don't need to make guns and munitions no more". He said this with a glumness that I was not used to. I know he was trying to be kind. In the army we dealt with serious situations by making a joke. It seemed in civvy street they dealt with it by being miserable. I thought I'm going to miss the army. I told dad that we had been told we would be returning to a land fit for heroes. He said, "Is that what they told you?"

To lighten the mood dad said, "Come on bor (boy), let's go down the Golden Star (Pub in St. Georges Street, Norwich) and have a jar". So we both went off, father and son, to the pub. It was good to talk with my dad who was usually quite quiet, albeit a bit strange, as we had not seen each other for 10 years. It was like the army had said it would be, we had left as boys and come home as men. I did notice that in the pub they were not laughing and larking about like I was used to. The atmosphere was sober and serious and people seemed a bit worried about things. The yards had changed. As a boy, despite the poverty, I remembered them as happy places. Now they seemed more serious places. The yards had changed. But then maybe, so had I.

As I went to sleep that night I remember thinking I had sort of come home, but hadn't. It was not what I had imagined it would be. The army had been where I had felt at home. Ringing in my head was what my dad said to me in the pub, "Don't talk about the war, no one is interested in that, that's the past - just get yourself a job."

11

THE MARCH ALONE

… the peaceful day at a Norfolk Cottage.

Marching as a postman, delivering kindness through Norfolk doors.

"So I became a postman, and while I was alone;
Each day I would deliver kindness, to a Norfolk home.
And through each mile, I would smile, as I'd come so far;
At day's end, I would, 'have-a-jar', in the Golden Star.

I then had a few years when I marched alone. Like many of the lads returning we found the next few years tough. Some lads kept asking themselves what was all the fighting for? But I did not find this helpful. We got a lot of support from The Regiment and the new Royal British Legion, but others outside the army did not seem to understand, or even care. Eventually I found a job that was right up my street .... a postman. I really enjoyed being a postman. I could spend most of the time marching, but this time rather than delivering terror we were delivering kindness through Norfolk doors. The days of the bad news telegrams had stopped. There were not the six deliveries a day we used to get before the war, but still plenty for us to do. Some of the boys in the factory or the street corner had it bad, but I was paid to walk in the fresh air and chat to nice people and deliver things that people were looking forward to getting. It seemed at the start as if I was marching alone but as the years passed, the posties became my new band of brothers. I had a new set of mates, and like the army, we looked out for each other.

The day I am going to tell you about is one when I changed from my normal round. I walked up the garden path to a beautiful cottage with red roses round the door, surrounded by a wild flower garden. As I arrived a lady opened the door. "Mornin" I said. She scowled at me and said nothing. I took a glance into her kitchen and could see hanging on the wall next to the Aga (cooker), pictures of three boys in uniform that looked about my age. I took it from what was hanging off the pictures, that they were no longer with us. She saw me looking at the pictures and said, "Where were you?" I replied, "Mesopotamia". There was a long pause and she stared past me. "Never heard of it" she said. Then she added, "They are in France .... you had it easy". She took the post from my hand, and then shut the door.

I thought about knocking and telling her about the siege, the death march, the concentration camp and all, but then as my dad said, no-one was really interested, and it would not help her with her loss. I dwelled on the fact that she emphasised ARE in France, but course really meaning they were dead and not coming home. I walked back down the path and reaching the end, I saw the bright colours of the flowers in the garden and being carried on the air, a sweet smell of honeysuckle and some bees, buzzing around it. It was a wonderful English summer morning. I stopped to look at the red roses, roses grown in a cottage garden in England ... they looked brilliant.

"'Scews me Mister", came a voice. A boy, looking about 11 years old, had also stopped on the track the other side of the wall to view the bees. He looked a bit like my younger brother Bertie. He asked, "Were you in the war?" He did not seem to have got the message that you were not supposed to talk about it. "Yes I was" I said. I asked him where he was from, and he said he was from Burley Street but before that, the yards in Norwich. "I'm from the yards", I said. He smiled. Looking at the bees, the boy said, "They are wonderful". I said "Yes, life is". I asked him, "What are you going to do when you grow up?" He said, "Well I've told my sister Go-Go (her name), that I am going to be a soldier." "That's good" I said, "You should tell Go-Go you want to join the Norfolks. Some people say there will not be much call for soldiering now that we have had the 'war to end all wars', but I'm not so sure". I saw the boy was listening intently so I continued... "But whatever you do, work hard, and try your best to enjoy it. Be disciplined and try to help others, and serve a greater purpose. At times it will get tough. But remember the boys from the yards cannot be beaten, and you should march on".

The boy said, "In the war, who were you with?" I paused, and then said proudly: "I was with 2 NORFOLK". They boy said "Who were they?" I paused again, and staring at the bees I said "They were the boys from the Norwich yards .... They were ..." I looked up ... and the boy had gone ...

THE END, OF 11 DAYS.

Imagined voice of Private Albert Edward Cushion, 7983

Norfolkman, Soldier, Postman and Familyman.
One of the one-in-ten who came home from Kut.
A good soldier and a good man, who lived a good life.
1892-1958

THANKS, RESEARCH AND ACKNOWLEDGEMENTS

I would like to thank all those that have helped me imagine, research and check this project. Particular thanks go to the Officers and men of the modern descendant unit of 2 NORFOLK, The Royal Anglian Regiment. Special thanks to the staff of the Royal Norfolk Regimental Museum, for the conversations; access to diaries, photographs, manuscript and orders, especially the records of Major (later Lt Col.) FC Lodge, and Capt. (later Major) AJ Shakeshaft. Also thanks to Norfolk County Council Museums Service; and Library and Information Service. During this research I was privileged to meet Martin Kearney, grandson of another 'Kuttie', 'Paddy' Kearney. I thank military historians Paul Knight (Mesopotamia) and Neil Storey (Norfolk Regiment) for their help, encouragement and support. I would also like to thank those that have helped with the production: my assistants Alison Dawson and Gus Plater; Mark and all the gang at Hollinger Print; Lt. Col (Ret'd) Mark Nicholas, Amy March, Charlie Watson, and all those who provided testimonies. Anything I have got right, is mainly thanks to all of the above. Anything I have not, and all errors, are my responsibility.

I have used the following books and material:

"Recollections of the Siege of Kut and After. Two Accounts by Indian Army Officers during the First World War in Mesopotamia". C.H. Barber and H.C.W Bishop. 2018.

"The Siege. The full, horrifying account of the Kut disaster". R. Braddon. 1969.

"The Royal Norfolk Regiment". T. Carew. 1967.

"Kut 1916. The forgotten British Disaster in Iraq". P. Crowley. 2009.

"The British Army in Mesopotamia, 1914-1918". P. Knight. 2013.

"The History of the Norfolk Regiment, 4th August 1914 to 31st December 1918". F. Loraine Petre. 2015.

"The secrets of a Kuttite: an authentic story of Kut, adventures in captivity and Stamboul intrigue". Capt. E.O. Mousley. 1922.

"Norfolk in the Great War. A Pictorial History". N. R. Storey. 2008.

"The Holy Boys. A History of the Royal Norfolk Regiment and The Royal East Anglian Regiment 1685-2010". J. Sutherland and D. Canwell. 2010.

"Battles on the Tigris. The Mesopotamian Campaign of the First World War". R. Wilcox. 2006.

Film: Letters from Baghdad. 2017 (The story of Iraq and Gertrude Bell).

Journal: "The Siege of Kut-al-Amara" By a linesman. Chambers' Journal, July 1936. Courtesy of Martin Kearney.

Online:

Broadcast: Voices of the First World War – Mesopotamia. Imperial War Museum. https://www.iwm.org.uk/VoicesOfTheFirstWorldWar. 2019.

Norfolk in World War One. www.norfolkinworldwar1.org. 2019.

Various Google searches on the historical detail.

Photographic acknowledgements:

Front cover and page 27: © Neil Storey Archive
Page 3: © Royal Norfolk Regimental Museum
Page 17: © Nigel Cushion
Page 19: © Nigel Cushion
Page 23: © Nigel Cushion
Page 34: © Royal Norfolk Regimental Museum
Page 37: Unable to find source to acknowledge
Page 44: © Robert Hunt Library / Mary Evans
Page 48: © Mary Evans / Sueddeutsche Zeitung Photo
Page 54: Unable to find source to acknowledge
Page 58: © Norfolk County Council Library and Information Service
Page 61: © Stuart Monk / Shuttershock
Page 69: © Nigel Cushion
Page 74: © Nigel Cushion
Page 79: © Nigel Cushion

Finally, thanks to my family:

My co-researcher and brother Paul Michael Cushion, pictured right, also of course, grandson of Albert Edward.

Our Uncle Albert aged 91, pictured centre, son of Albert Edward.

Our dad, Michael George Cushion (1936-2012), also son of Albert Edward, who had much of Albert Edward's spirit, and who lovingly passed it on to us.

100 years on. Nigel Cushion, Uncle Albert and Paul Cushion, 2019.

LEADERSHIP LESSONS

I did not realise when I started the research for this book that it would be such a revealing and inspiring journey for me. Having spent most of the last 35 years of my working life studying and practicing leadership and working closely with leaders, I came to reflect on what leadership lessons this story might have revealed. What can the adventures of Albert and the lads from the yards teach us about leadership? Here are 11 lessons. I have crafted them as 11 challenges or tests, from the 11 days. How many of these challenges can you meet?

1. The first job of a leader is to create an atmosphere of a band of brothers, imbued with a belief that "we" is greater than "I", and in the belief that you are both expected to do your best and that you are the best. It is a blend of pride, humility, professionalism and discipline, with a sense of history and a sense of the present.

   The Right of the Line Challenge. As leader, have you created an atmosphere of a band of brothers?

2. Leaders come in all shapes and sizes. Leadership transcends race, colour, creed, nationality and time, but we live in tribes and often see others as "them". However bridges can be built to cross the separation river, and they are often built out of humour and friendship.

   The Mo Challenge. As leader, do you build bridges to reach out and connect with those not in your tribe?

3. Most of the time it's business as usual, but at some point we will all face "Shaiba days". On these days when you are facing overwhelming odds, you will need to commit everything you have to win the day. This might be on the battlefield or in the boardroom; on the sports field or in a start-up company; in public service or on your personal journey in life. On these days the real leaders need to find courage, and step to the front of the trench and draw their sword. You cannot lead from the rear.

   The Shaiba Challenge. When it really counts, do you have the courage to step forward at personal risk and lead from the front?

4. Leadership often comes from those in leadership positions. But it can also come too from your peers, your family and your friends. We can be hugely inspired by those we are closest to. We often do not realise this until after they have gone.

   Smitty's Challenge. Do you seek leadership inspiration from, and offer it to, your family, friends and peers?

5. Leadership is a riddle, wrapped in a mystery, inside an enigma (borrowed from Churchill). Leadership is about the leader, but great leaders know it's more about their followers. Usually the needs of the followers and the leader align. But if they don't, the best leaders put the needs of their followers before themselves.

   The Townsend Challenge. When your needs and the needs of your followers diverge, do you put their needs before your own?

6. Sometimes despite your best efforts, you will not win. But that is not the same as being defeated. The leader needs to accept this and teach this to their followers. The leader and followers need to be able to look each other in the eye and know that both have given of their best.

   The Kut Challenge. After a loss, can you look your followers in the eye and know, that all have given their best?

7. Sometimes things turn from bad to worse, and all hope seems to be lost. When this happens, the leader's job is remind everyone who "we" are.

   The Desert March Challenge. As leader, can you face the reality of where you are, yet lift morale by reminding the followers who "we" are?

8. At the heart of great leadership is a sacred relationship between the leader and those who willingly follow them. It cannot be fully understood by those who were not there.

   The Unspoken Challenge. Show respect for the sacred bond between the leader and the followers.

9. Leadership is about caring for those who choose to follow you, winning their respect, and getting them home.

   The 'Charlie' Aldridge Challenge. As leader, have you won the respect of your followers and do they know you care for them?

10. Leadership changes us, and good leadership changes us for good. We cannot return to where and who we were before.

The Coming Home Challenge. Accept that leadership changes us. March on.

11. Leadership is about your followers being part of a "they". Theys are created when spirit is released, and extraordinary performance is delivered from ordinary people. This is the legacy of leadership.

The "They" Challenge. When you are long gone as a leader, will they talk with admiration about the "they" you created?

THE POEM "THEY"

Imagined voice of Private Albert E Cushion. 2 NORFOLK.
Written on 11/11 2018 by his grandson Nigel Cushion.
100 years from the end of The Great War.

Who were they? Albert is third row from the top, third man in.

THEY

They said, you should join the army boy,
They said, the Norfolk's are for you.
Go you up to Britannia Barracks,
And your mates will be there too.

They sent us on a great adventure,
The King's business was in hand.
They sent us off to India,
And then the promised land.

We ended up in Mesopotamia,
They said we made lots of noise.
They marched us up the Tigris,
They called us the "holy boys".

They said we fought very well,
They said we couldn't be beaten.
But then we got a bloody nose,
Our concern was what we'd eaten!

The Indian boys had it worse,
As they could not eat horse.
Don't worry lads, a few more days,
"Stiff upper lip" of course.

Day 147.
They said we had to surrender,
Is this what the British Army do?
When they ordered "destroy all arms",
Most of us, were on the loo!

With relief just miles away,
They said they saw our smoke.
We kept the humour going,
The lads love a joke.

But while we were laughing,
The relief O/C cried.
We knew, like us, they'd done their best,
At least they had tried.

They said it's worse than Yorktown,
Would our action be misunderstood?
Only three-in-ten would make it through,
We did the best we could.

They said we were their prisoners,
To us they were not kind.
They forced us on a death march,
The fight was in our mind.

They stole from us, stoned us, starved us,
Killed the sick, when we fell.
Made us march 1000 miles,
To a desert hell.

They made us build a railway,
Concentration camp ... 2-year.
Had we been forgotten?
Did anybody care?

In 1918
They said it was all over,
They said it's now all done.
They said they could not break us,
And told us that we'd won.

The 2nds mustered at the boat,
The RSM, had a pen.
Of battalion strength that disembarked,
We now had one-in-ten.

In 1919
They welcomed us back to Norwich,
The real promised land.
They marched us up to City Hall,
Flags waving in their hand.

They called us heroes,
They said they'd done the sums.
They said of all the holy boys,
We were the lucky ones.

They called it "war to end all wars",
They said it was now all done.
And then they discharged us,
No need for your gun.

But home had changed and so had we,
There was no time to be kind.
We looked around the Norfolk homes,
Not the ones we left behind.

They said we were a "band of brothers"
But Bertie is not here.
They told us to forget it,
Did they really care?

They said it's time to move on,
No more marching now you're home.
Our hardest fight was yet to come,
This time we marched alone.

So I became a postman, and while I was alone,
Each day I would deliver kindness, to a Norfolk home.
And through each mile, I would smile, as I'd come so far,
At day's end, I would, 'have-a-jar', in the Golden Star.

In years to come if they ask …. "tell us who were THEY"?
Tell them ... they were the holy boys, who went Asiatic way.
They were the boys who fought their way, all the way, through hell,
They were the boys who have a story, that is yet to tell.
They were the boys who did their best, who marched-on beyond their limit,
They were the boys from the Norwich yards, with undefeatable spirit.

We do not need your sympathy and certainly no fuss…
But maybe, in 100 years … they will remember us?

REMEMBERED.

MARCHING ON

The spirit of the boys at Kut marches on. It marches on through their blood descendants.

It marches on, through the descendant military units of The Royal Anglian Regiment, specifically A (Norfolk) Company of the 1st Battalion, and Number 1 (Norfolk) Company of the 3rd Battalion. We need to make sure we look after those coming home in the future better than we did in the past, so a percentage of the profits from this book will be given to charities supporting the welfare of current and former members of these units to help them march on.

The spirit can march on through you. Whenever you are facing overwhelming odds. Be it on the battlefield or in the boardroom; on the sports field or in a start-up company; in public service or on your personal journey in life. Remember the lads at Kut. Remember the boys from the yards. Remember the spirit they had. I believe we can all have this spirit. But you cannot release it on your own, you will need to surround yourself with others who have it.

It is born out of humility and humour. It is forged in the furnace where overwhelming odds are met with leadership, courage, professionalism and discipline, and an unshakeable belief that you cannot be beaten. It is called undefeatable spirit.